MY MISCHIEVOUS WHEELCHAIR

by Molly David

Illustrated by Solomiia at GetYourBookIllustrations

Text and Illustrations copyright © 2023 Molly David

Published by Semper Grata (Sempergrata.com)
For orders, please visit www.mollydavidauthor.com

All rights reserved.
No part of this publication may be reproduced, distributed, or transmitted in any form or by any means, including photocopying, recording, or other electronic or mechanical methods, without the prior written permission of the publisher, except in the case of brief quotations embodied in reviews and certain other noncommercial uses permitted by copyright law.
The moral right of the author and illustrator has been asserted.

Illustrated by Solomiia at GetYourBookIllustrations
Cover and Book Design by Kezia at GetYourBookIllustrations
www.getyourbookillustrations.com

Hardback ISBN-13: 978-1-957696-26-3
Paperback ISBN-13: 978-1-957696-27-0
eBook ISBN-13: 978-1-957696-25-6

Library of Congress Control Number: 2023917312

David, Molly
My Mischievous Wheelchair / Molly David
Grace is working hard to win Student of the Month. Her wheelchair temporarily derails her plans when it decides it is not getting enough attention. Grace's wheelchair takes over her day and will not behave until it gets what it wants.
A humorous story about a wheelchair that refuses to be ignored and the mischief it creates. A fun twist on how society sees people with disabilities. It is an engaging, fun, and active story for children ages 4-8.

First Print 2023

Dedication

My daughter, Reagan, the strongest person I know and who deserves to see books that represent her, inspired this book.

To my daughter, Chloe, whose bravery and kindness make the world a better place.

And to my husband, Donald, who makes my world better. 143.

Grace squirmed in her seat. The Student of the Month award would be hers. She could already see the certificate hanging on her bedroom wall. Her parents would shower her with gifts, and her sister would be green with envy.

The librarian reminded Grace that being on time is important.

"It's not me; it's my chair."

She was worried the chair's behavior would ruin her chance to become Student of the Month.

She was getting madder and madder at her chair.

"I didn't mean to hurt you, Grace. Everyone notices you and talks to you, but nobody notices me or interacts with me. That hurts my feelings."

Grace didn't realize the chair felt left out. She wanted to make this better.

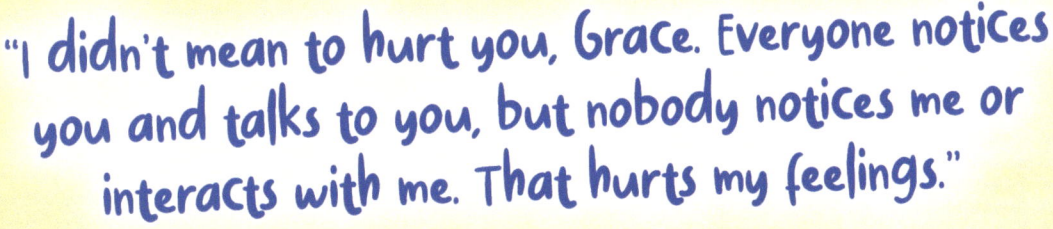

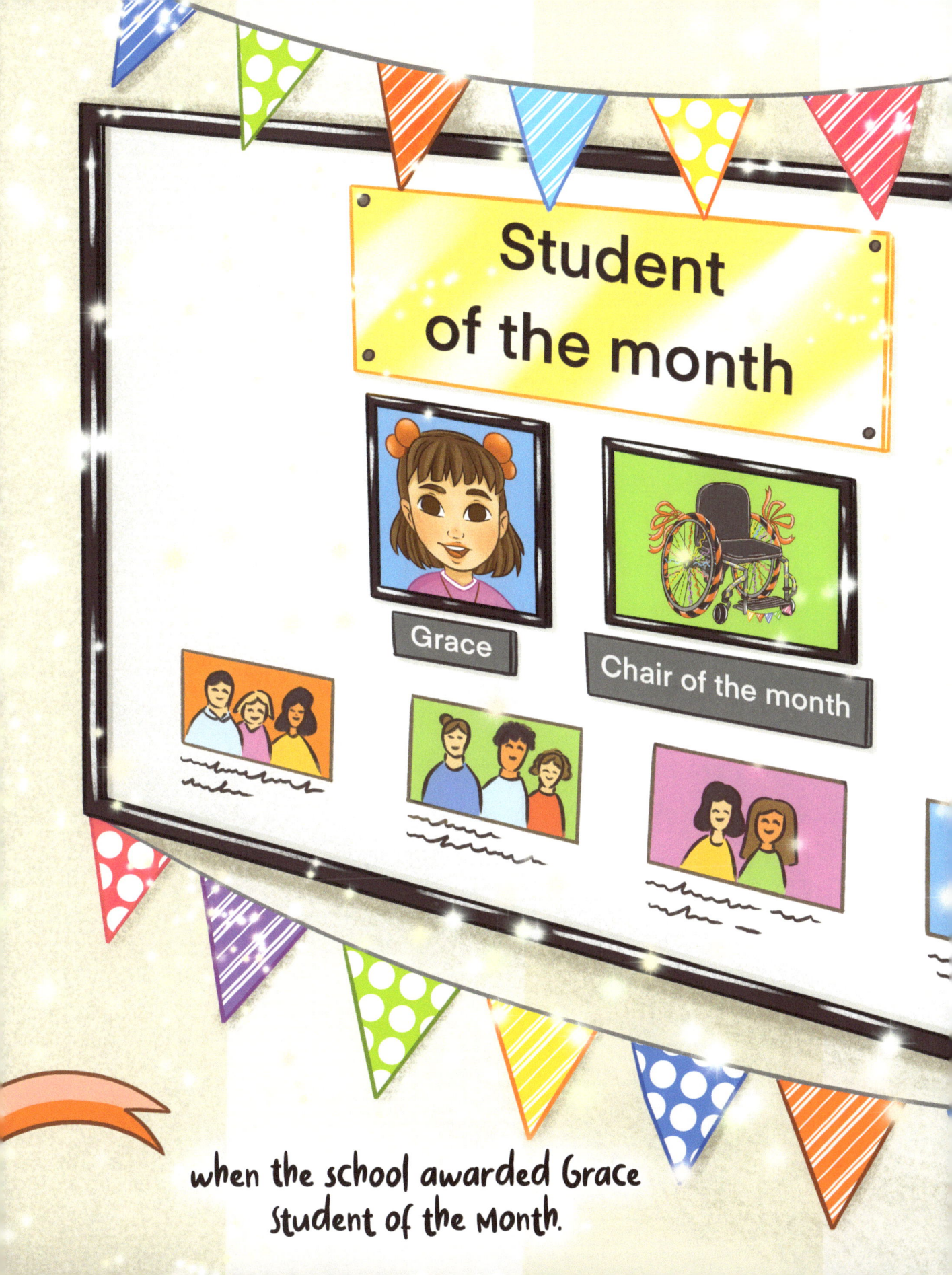

when the school awarded Grace
Student of the Month.

About the Author

Molly David writes and presents on disability issues. As the mother of a child with a disability, Molly understands the importance of diversity in children's books. Molly David authored the book *Planning for the Future: Protecting a Loved One with a Disability* and various news outlets like The Associated Press, nerdwallet, and wealth of Geeks have interviewed her for articles.

Molly is a retired teacher who lives in Farmington Hills, MI with her husband, two daughters, and two dogs. She spends too much of her time searching for her phone and watching dog videos online. Molly would love to connect with you through her website, Instagram, or Facebook, especially if you have dog videos.

mollydavidauthor.com
@mollydavidauthor
mollydavidauthor

Printed in the USA
CPSIA information can be obtained
at www.ICGtesting.com
LVHW071945011123
762649LV00019B/758